CA
COCKER SPANIELS

By Becky Corwin-Adams

Published by Brittdog Publishing

Cast-Off Cocker Spaniels by Becky Corwin-Adams

Published by Brittdog Publishing

Publishers Cataloging In Publication Data Available Upon Request

ISBN: 978-1482070118

TABLE OF CONTENTS

DEDICATION

*T*his book is dedicated to Columbus Cocker Rescue and the wonderful group of volunteers who have worked tirelessly to find furever homes for more than 1,200 homeless cocker spaniels. Many of the dogs featured in this book are Columbus Cocker Rescue alumni.

Columbus Cocker Rescue is a non-profit 501(c)(3) organization operated solely on volunteer support and donations. Our mission is to provide rescue for at-risk cocker spaniels in the greatest need. Cockers are rescued from high-kill shelters, puppy mills, and other dangerous situations, in and around the Ohio area.

A portion of the proceeds from this book will be donated to Columbus Cocker Rescue.

To find out how you can help, visit our web page:

www.columbuscockerrescue.org

INTRODUCTION

My first pet was a red cocker spaniel named Ginger. My parents were still newlyweds when they "rescued" Ginger from a relative. They lived in an upstairs apartment at the time.

By the time I was born, my parents and my older sister had moved into a house. Ginger was eight years old, and she had become an outside dog. Ginger had also had a litter of puppies, courtesy of a neighborhood dog running loose.

When I was a young child, my parents suspected that I had allergies, so I was not allowed to be around Ginger. Extensive allergy testing proved that I was not allergic to Ginger or anything else.

Winters in Ohio were very cold, and Ginger was sometimes allowed to come into the house. I loved waking up in the morning to be greeted by Ginger. She used to drink her water out of a flat, one-pound Maxwell House coffee can.

Ginger passed away at the age of 13. I was five years old at the time. I remember my mom being very upset. She made it clear that we could never have another dog, after the heartbreak of Ginger's passing. We had dozens of cats over the years, along with a guinea pig, a hamster, a gerbil, a mouse, chickens, and goldfish.

Randy and I had been married for 20 years and had never had a pet, except a hamster that only lived for a week or two. Our two sons had graduated high school and gone into college.

While spending a week in Iowa with my niece, Randy and I fell in love with her cocker spaniel, Francie. We decided we needed a dog to help combat the empty nest syndrome. Since my childhood dog had been a cocker spaniel, we definitely wanted a cocker.

We didn't know anything about dog rescue at the time. We were not looking for a puppy. We had already potty-trained two children and were not interested in training a puppy. We also did not want to spend hundreds of dollars for a dog.

We called the Defiance County (Ohio) Humane Society and put our name on the waiting list. We asked for a young, buff female cocker spaniel. We thought we might have to wait a long time to find the dog we wanted.

A week later, we got a call from the Humane Society. They had a young, buff female cocker spaniel, an owner surrender.

BRITTANY, THE DEVIL DOG

*W*e went to Defiance County Humane Society to see the dog, whose name was Brittany.

The cocker did not fit the picture of the dog I had in mind. Even though Brittany really looked like a shaggy mutt, we decided to take her home with us. She was very thin, about 21 pounds, and needed a haircut. She certainly wasn't a show dog.

When we arrived home, we opened the car door in our driveway, and Brittany took off running. We chased her down the street. When we called her by name, she responded. Brittany happily ran around inside the house until bedtime. We put her in a crate in the garage, and she whined for several hours. We finally let her out of the crate, and she promptly ran into our bedroom, jumped on our bed, and fell asleep. Brittany slept on our bed every night after that.

Brittany was 15 months old. She had lived with a single man since she was a puppy. We talked to the previous owner to find out more about our new dog. He had fed Brittany pizza and chicken and allowed her to sleep on his bed. He had never taken her to a vet to get shots or had her groomed. His girlfriend had moved in, along with her two cats, and since Brittany did not like cats at all, the man had taken her to the Humane Society.

Brittany loved pizza. When we ordered a pizza, we had to put her outside so that we could eat without her begging and trying to steal the pizza. She also loved lasagna. Once, our son called her name, and instead of running to him, Brittany ran over to the table and jumped right into a plate of lasagna.

Brittany started to gain weight at our house. She got lots of treats and had dozens of toys to play with. We had a fenced yard, but we quickly found out that Brittany could easily climb over the chain link fence. Our son took Brittany outside to teach her to chase and retrieve a tennis ball. He threw the ball in one direction, and Brittany took off running in the other direction and climbed the fence. Our son kicked off his sandals, jumped the fence, and ran after her.

We decided Brittany needed to be tethered, so we bought a tie-out for her. A few days later, we came home and Brittany was missing. A note on our door informed us that Brittany had decided to visit the cocker spaniels down the street. She had broken her collar and climbed the fence again. We bought her a sturdier collar.

Brittany had her spay surgery done a few weeks later. When we brought her home, I was sure she would not run off with stitches in her belly. Once again, Brittany climbed the fence and ran. Later that day, she started chewing on the stitches until she had removed most of them. Luckily, she stopped chewing before she did major damage to herself.

Brittany also learned how to jump up and bump the latch on our screen door, so it would open. One day, she took off out the front door. I grabbed her leash and a dog biscuit and followed her. I found her in the yard next door. She was sitting on top of our very surprised, bikini-clad neighbor, who had been asleep in a lounge chair. Brittany was licking the lady's face. The neighbor informed me that my dog was loose, as if I always walked around carrying a leash and a dog biscuit. I apologized and took Brittany home. After that, Brittany's nickname was "Houdini."

We left Brittany at home one day when we had to go out of town. Our son came over to check on her. Brittany was not supposed to be in the house. She almost knocked our son down when he opened the front door. We discovered a cocker-spaniel-sized hole chewed through our screen door. Brittany had been sleeping on our bed while we were gone.

We left Brittany at the kennel the next time we went out of town. When I went to pick her up, the lady referred to her as "The Devil Dog." I asked what Brittany had done to earn that title, and no one would tell me. I never did find out. She now had her second nickname: "Devil Dog."

Brittany loved to destroy pillows. She chewed up every decorative pillow we had. She also chewed up all of her stuffed toys. I would put the stuffing back in and sew up the holes, until the toy was no longer able to be saved. Brittany chewed her favorite leash in half one day. The leash said, "I Love My Cocker Spaniel." I did not love her very much that day!

Brittany hated a lilac bush we had in our back yard. Every time she walked past it, she would try to attack the bush. One day Brittany broke off a six-inch-long branch and got it stuck in her mouth. I tried for 10 minutes to dislodge it. I finally called Randy at work, and he quickly came home. It took both of us to get the branch out of her mouth.

Our son thought it would be fun to get Brittany a huge rawhide bone for Christmas. She carried it around the house, scratching and banging the walls. Brittany later choked on a piece of a rawhide chew toy. Randy quickly performed the Heimlich maneuver and was able to dislodge the piece of rawhide. That was the last time Brittany ever got a rawhide toy.

Brittany hated water. She quickly learned that we only took showers, never a bath. If she heard us filling the bathtub with water, Brittany knew it was for her. She would run and hide. You could never use the word "bath" around her. Once she was finally in the tub, if you turned your back on her, she would jump out and run back to her favorite hiding place.

One evening Randy and I were sitting in the hot tub. It was dark out, and we each had a wine cooler. I heard a splash and thought my wine cooler had fallen into the hot tub. I quickly tried to find it in the water. Instead, I was very surprised to find a wet cocker spaniel! Brittany had jumped in. I think she was as surprised as we were. A wet dog smells bad, but a dog that has been soaked in a chemically treated hot tub smells worse. She only tried that trick one time.

We also had an above-ground pool. Brittany would climb up on the hot tub cover and sleep in the sun while we were in the pool. She could see us from that vantage point. Our son accused her of breaking the hot tub cover, which was impossible, since Brittany didn't weigh very much.

Brittany would sometimes climb up the pool ladder to see what we were doing. One time I carried her into the pool with me. As soon as she saw the water, she got frightened. Brittany dug her sharp claws into my chest. I was screaming, Brittany was hanging onto me, and Randy was laughing. That cocker definitely did not like water.

Our son's pug, Sairhe, would come to visit, and she loved the pool. Sairhe was content to float around the pool on an air mattress. Not Brittany!

We decided Brittany might be happier if she had a playmate. We took a female cocker spaniel named Buffy on a home trial visit. Brittany scared the poor dog and wanted to fight with her. After a few hours, we returned Buffy to her owner. We found out later that Brittany hated all other female dogs. She would try to attack them, even if they were walking on the opposite side of the street.

We did find a male cocker spaniel who received the Brittany "Seal of Approval," so we adopted Bubba. They got along fine, since Bubba quickly learned that Brittany was the boss.

Brittany was terrified of mirrors. I held her up to a mirror one day, and when she saw her reflection, Brittany went crazy trying to get the "other dog." She did not like other dogs, and she had no idea that it was herself she was trying to attack!

We took Brittany on a lot of long walks in other cities and states. The first time we took Brittany along, our friend Thelma was very excited to meet her. We had explained to Thelma that Brittany did not like other female dogs. Thelma opened the car door, took Brittany out, and tried to introduce her to another female dog. We quickly had an altercation on our hands.

Brittany opened most of the Christmas gifts under our tree. We discovered that she was fascinated by ribbons and bows. She especially loved the red bows, even though I was told that dogs are colorblind. Not Brittany! We stopped making the presents look so nice, and Brittany left them alone.

Brittany had occasional seizures. One evening we were walking when she had a seizure in the middle of the street. We picked her up and moved her to the grass. There was a sign in the yard that said, "No Dogs." The homeowner came outside to see why there was a dog in his yard. When I explained that the poor dog was having a seizure, the man stomped back into his house. He obviously was not a dog person!

Brittany became deaf when she was nine years old, so we taught her American Sign Language. Brittany also lost control of her bladder. She loved to sit on my lap. She would fall asleep, and all of a sudden, I would be very wet. She did the same thing when she slept with us at night.

Brittany was definitely a learning experience, since she was our first dog. We made a lot of mistakes training her. Even though some people called her "Devil Dog," we just called her "Brittdog."

BUBBA, A FARM DOG

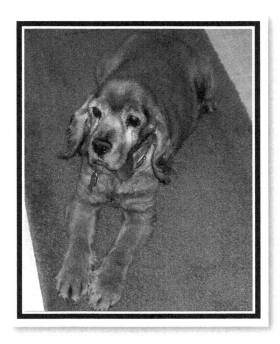

We saw an ad in a local farm newspaper advertising a red male cocker spaniel for sale. I had always wanted a red cocker spaniel, since Ginger, my childhood cocker, was red. We went to the owner's farm to look at the dog.

The two-year-old male cocker spaniel desperately needed a haircut. He had big mats of fur all over his body. He looked like a miniature reddish-brown bear. His name was Cinnamon. He had never had any shots or even been taken to see a vet, according to his owner. The dog was allowed to roam free, eating whatever birds and small animals he could kill.

Cinnamon had been passed from home to home, and this farm was his fourth home in his short lifetime. His mother, his sister, and four other female dogs all lived in a muddy pen behind the old farmhouse. Cinnamon had been born on this farm, rehomed twice, and then returned to the farm, all in a period of two years. The owners evidently cropped his tail, because it was almost non-existent. Sometimes it looked like he didn't even have a tail, depending on the way he was standing.

We thought about the dog for a few days. We decided to take our Brittany to meet him and let her make the final decision. Brittany did not like very many dogs. When she met this dog, it was love at first sight.

We took the dog home and named him Beauford, after a character in the movie *Forrest Gump*. Our young granddaughter could not say his name, so Beauford soon became known as Bubba.

We took him to visit our vet. The next day, we learned that Bubba had heartworm disease. It had been caught at an early stage, and the vet was very optimistic about the treatment. The vet tried a new, experimental heartworm treatment. We had to keep Bubba quiet for six weeks, and he made a full recovery.

The morning after the vet pronounced him heartworm-free, we took Bubba for a walk. He managed to slip out of his collar. Bubba ran and ran, across the road and through a field. He ran in circles, never getting close enough for us to catch him. Finally, Bubba made one more loop and slid across the wet grass, landing at my feet. He had managed to use up all of the energy he had been storing up for the past six weeks.

We kept Bubba in our back yard for a while. We were not sure if he was housebroken. Every time we brought him in the house, he would leave his mark on a beanbag chair. We were never quite sure if it was the chair he didn't like or the team logo that was on the chair.

One night we had torrential rain. In the middle of the night, we woke up and went out to check on Bubba. He was sitting on top of his doghouse, which was surrounded by several inches of water. We carried Bubba into the house and dried him off. He ended up spending that night inside. Soon, he was spending every night inside the house, claiming his space on our bed.

Bubba liked to sleep in the bathroom, too. He would push the door shut with his nose. When he wanted out, he would whine until someone opened the door for him.

Bubba hated riding in the car. He would pace around the back seat and whine. We moved halfway across the state when Bubba was about 10 years old. The entire three-hour trip was filled with Bubba whining and pacing. He finally settled down and fell asleep as we were getting off the interstate at our exit.

Bubba starting having seizures when he was five years old. He had to take pills twice a day to prevent them. Later, he had several surgeries to remove cancerous growths: one from his eye, one from his stomach, and several from his ears.

Bubba had extensive ear surgery and eventually became deaf. He already knew American Sign Language, since Brittany was also deaf. Bubba responded very well to sign language. His favorite signs were "eat" and "walk." He always knew when we were getting his food ready. He would be sound asleep in another room and come running as soon as he sensed the food bag being rattled.

Bubba also suffered from severe allergies. He was so itchy that he would walk under the furniture and scratch his back against it. Bubba knocked over our kitchen table one time. Another time, he managed to move the table halfway across the room. He knocked over an end table and a lamp too many times to count.

Bubba developed cataracts later in life. He had a swayed back from an improperly healed injury early in his life. Bubba had been mistreated before we adopted him. He was terrified of ropes and sticks.

Bubba loved bugs. He would catch cicadas and locusts in our back yard. He did not even bother to kill them. He just swallowed them alive, in one gulp. You could still hear them buzzing inside of him.

Bubba never played with toys. He was not at all destructive. He never chewed or destroyed anything. He liked to give kisses. He would give you several kisses in a row. Then, when you least expected it, he would act like he was going to give you a kiss. Instead, he would nip at the end of your nose. It was just a gentle nip that didn't really hurt. It just took the recipient by surprise.

Bubba led a very active life. He loved to go for walks. He was a farm dog turned city dog. He never lost his hunting instinct. He often killed baby rabbits in our yard. Bubba loved road kill – the deader, the better. One time he found a flattened dead squirrel and picked it up while we were walking. He proudly carried it in his mouth until we were able to persuade him to drop it. Another time, Bubba picked up a dead bird. We tried to make him drop it. Instead, he got it farther into his mouth until only the bird's legs were visible. Another of Bubba's favorite delicacies was dead frogs.

You can take a dog out of the country, but you can't take the country out of the dog!

***

AWARD-WINNING DOG

Bubba was an award-winning dog. The year after we adopted him, he was chosen to be a calendar dog. He was featured on one of the pages of Day Dream's Day in a Box Dog Calendar.

Bubba was also chosen as "Dog of the Year" at our local Wal-mart. He received a certificate and several edible prizes. My essay explaining how Bubba came to live with us and how he overcame heartworm disease was selected as the grand prize winner.

Our vet, Dr. Brent Pettigrew of Fountain City Veterinary Hospital in Bryan, Ohio, always called Bubba "The Miracle Dog." He would often tell one of his new staff members the story of Bubba's heartworm treatment. The intranasal drug Dr. Pettigrew used to treat Bubba was new. Although the treatment was successful, Dr. Pettigrew vowed to never use the drug to treat another dog because Bubba had become so aggressive while he was administering it.

Bubba did show his appreciation to Dr. Pettigrew for saving his life. As I was talking to the doctor one day, Bubba lifted his leg on the doctor's pant leg. By the time I noticed, it was too late. I was very embarrassed. It was as if one of my children had just done a bad thing. The doctor just laughed.

A few months later, I noticed that the carpet at the Vet Hospital had been replaced with tile. I imagine Bubba was not the only dog to have left his mark on that carpet.

BARKLEY, THE DOG WITH THE TAIL

We were not looking for another cocker spaniel, but when we took our granddaughter to the Defiance County Humane Society to look for a Dalmatian, we saw Barkley.

Barkley had been found roaming the city streets. He had been at the Humane Society for four months. He had been adopted once and returned the next morning. The family accused Barkley of growling at their children. Fortunately, this is a no-kill shelter.

Barkley was a buff-and-white cocker spaniel with very droopy eyes and a long tail. It had never been docked, like most cocker spaniel tails are. His tail would go around in circles when he was happy. Most people called him "the dog with the tail."

Barkley's photo appeared in an adoption ad in the local newspaper. We stopped by the shelter again, and Barkley was still there. We couldn't get those big, sad eyes out of our minds. Randy really wanted to adopt Barkley, even though we already had two cockers. I finally told him to do whatever he wanted to do about Barkley.

The next day when I got home from work, I looked out of the window and did a double take. There was Barkley, tied to the clothesline pole in our back yard.

The shelter staff had not given him a name, even though he had been there for more than four months. We decided to name him Barkley.

Barkley was very polite and well-behaved. He was the only cocker we ever had who did not try to take over our bed. Barkley preferred his own pillow on the floor. Barkley already knew several tricks when we adopted him. He knew how to roll over and how to stand up on his hind legs and beg. He would also "dance" on his hind legs, turning around in circles.

Barkley loved to walk. We are members of a walking club. We do a six-mile walk almost every weekend. Barkley usually went with us. Sometimes, we walked 12 miles in one day, and Barkley didn't mind. When we went away for a weekend of walking, Barkley went along. He traveled to Indiana, Michigan, and Illinois to walk.

One weekend, we went to Illinois to do some walking. After our walk, we went out for dinner. We left Barkley in his crate in the hotel room, thinking he would fall asleep. When we returned, we were told that there had been complaints about him. He was barking and bothering people. The hotel manager had gone into the room to check on him and had decided that Barkley needed the lights and the television on. That did not help, since Barkley never watched television at home.

After that, we left Barkley in the car when were going out for dinner. He was fine in the car. He was used to it, since he did so much traveling with us.

One very cold and rainy weekend, we walked in Indiana. Barkley was wet and shivering in the car. We took off our jackets and wrapped them around him, so he could warm up. Barkley had a huge burr stuck in the fur on his leg. We tried to remove it, but we were unsuccessful. We ended up cutting the burr out at home.

Barkley had a walking buddy, a female dog named Tootsie. Barkley got really excited when he saw Tootsie, and they walked very well together.

Unfortunately, Barkley developed arthritis. He gradually slowed down and started walking with a limp. He was on medication for the arthritis. One day, Barkley could not finish a walk. He had to be carried for the last three blocks. That was no easy feat, as Barkley was very tall and weighed 41 pounds. He was rather large for a cocker spaniel. He had long legs and very big paws.

Barkley always had a bad habit of eating things he shouldn't. He ate seashells, stones, and bark chips. He ate a beaded craft project. He also ate a suction cup and a plastic bottle cap.

When we went to Florida one winter, we left the dogs at the kennel. When we picked up the dogs, we noticed that Barkley was very lethargic. At first, we thought he was just tired from all of the excitement at the kennel. He didn't want to eat, which was extremely unusual for him. We got him to eat soft food, in small amounts. Since he had most of his teeth removed and the rest were bad, we thought he just couldn't chew the dry food anymore. We were not too concerned.

The following week, he ate less every day. We took Barkley to the vet. The vet did some blood tests. He thought the arthritis medication was causing a stomach problem, so he stopped the medication. He gave Barkley two new medications. That afternoon, Barkley vomited a three-inch-long splinter of wood. He fell down on the floor and just lay there for a few minutes. I called the vet's office and was told to make Barkley eat some Vaseline on a cotton ball, in case there were more splinters inside of him. Getting a dog to eat Vaseline is no easy task, especially when the dog is sick and grumpy.

When we got the test results back on Friday, Barkley's red blood cell count was half of what it should have been, and his white blood count was elevated. His protein level was low. The vet told us that Barkley was in "serious trouble." That was his polite way of telling us that Barkley might not survive the weekend. By Sunday, he was acting a little better and wanting to eat people food.

We visited the vet again. Barkley's red blood cell count had risen slightly. The vet thought the splinter of wood had caused bleeding in his stomach. Barkley had lost five pounds. He was sleeping all day and eating very little.

Barkley had another check-up and more blood tests. He was starting to hate going to the vet's office. I had to carry him to the exam room, since he refused to walk. He did get a better report, even though his red blood cell count was still low. He finally started eating his regular dog food again. He had lost two more pounds, for a total of seven. That little splinter of wood ended up costing us hundreds of dollars. It nearly cost Barkley his life.

Barkley finally rallied from that life-threatening incident. He was once again eating his food and all the treats he could get. He was able to take a few very short walks with us. His idea of a walk was to check out the fire hydrant in our front yard to see what other dogs had visited that day. After sniffing the area, Barkley was ready to go back to his pillow. He was not very active, but his tail always wagged when he saw us. Barkley would greet me at the door every day when I got home from work.

Some people still refer to Barkley as "the dog with the tail."

***

'TWAS A COLD NOVEMBER MORNING

A Poem for Barkley

'Twas a cold November morning, when all through
   the pound
Not a creature was stirring, not even a hound.
The nametags were hung by each kennel with care,
In hopes that a furever family soon would be there.

The dogs were nestled all snug in their beds,
While visions of a furever home danced in
   their heads.
Wishing and hoping for a nice warm lap,
The dogs settled down for a long winter's nap.

When out in the lobby there arose such a clatter,
They sprang from their beds to see what was
   the matter.
To the front of their kennels they flew like a flash,
Sliding into the doors with a loud crash.

The dogs lined their kennels, all in a row.
They barked and they whined and put on a show.
When, what to their wondering eyes should appear
But a friendly looking man, and his wife, so dear.

Past several kennels they walked, so quick,
Barkley knew it was time to do his best trick.
More rapid than eagles, to his kennel they came,
They nodded and smiled and called him by name.

"We'll take this one," the friendly man said,
As he patted dear Barkley on top of the head.
The man took a leash from a hook on the wall,
Fastened it on Barkley and led him down the hall.

Barkley wiped a tear from his eye,
As he gave his kennel mates a hasty goodbye.
To the office the kennel manager nearly flew,
Knowing he had paperwork to do.

As rain pounded on the shelter's roof,
Barkley let out a happy little woof.
He took one final look around,
And out the door they all went with a bound.

Barkley was prancing on nimble feet,
So happy was he, as he climbed in the back seat.
Barkley never once looked back
After the kind lady gave him a snack.

He settled down for the rest of the drive;
At his furever home he soon would arrive.
To Barkley's new house they did go,
His new yard was covered with light snow,

With some grass underneath,
And on the front door was a pine cone wreath.
Barkley loved his furever home,
With lots and lots of room to roam.

There was a dog bed, soft as a marshmallow,
Just the right size for the little fellow.
Barkley circled three times and laid down
    on the bed,
And he knew right away, there was nothing
    to dread.

Dreaming sweet dreams was easy work,
Suddenly, he awoke with a jerk.
A savory aroma greeted his nose
And up from his bed Barkley quickly arose.

The man called the dog with a loud whistle,
Barkley sprang to the kitchen just like a missile.
A tasty dinner was quite a welcome sight,
Barkley knew his furever home was just right!

BLACKIE, OUR FIRST FOSTER DOG

*B*rittany, our first cocker spaniel, passed away very suddenly. We were not ready to adopt another dog yet, but when a rescue asked us to foster a "two-year-old" black cocker spaniel, we agreed.

When we went to pick up the dog, we were surprised to see how small she was. We decided she was probably around eight months old. We had never adopted a dog as a puppy, so this one was going to be a real challenge!

The dog did not have a name. The rescue had been calling her "Cocker," so we named her Black Beauty. She was the biggest tomboy ever, so we started calling her Blackie.

Blackie was a very curious dog. She loved rope toys. Blackie liked to play tug of war for a few minutes, until she became bored. She was not content until she chewed the rope toy into dozens of little pieces.

Blackie loved to chew cords, too. She chewed on a heating pad while it was being used and then ran over to me, with a terrified expression on her little face. I noticed tooth marks on the cord. Blackie also chewed the cord to a computer mouse. She chewed it very neatly into six-inch-long pieces. She also chewed the strap off a briefcase. We soon learned to keep anything with a cord or strap out of her reach.

Blackie has her very own special aunt, our friend Thelma, who still refers to Blackie as "my niece." Auntie gives Blackie extra treats, even though she denies it. She always brings a new toy for Blackie when she comes to visit. Each time, Auntie says that she has found a great toy that Blackie cannot destroy. Within five minutes, the toy is in pieces. Auntie never has found a Blackie-proof toy.

Since Blackie had been abandoned by her previous owners, she has a problem with food. She loves to eat. Any time she can steal food from the table, she does. Blackie can often be found standing on the dining room table, looking for crumbs. She has never missed a meal at our house. Blackie still comes running any time she thinks someone has food.

Blackie is terrified of storms and vacuum cleaners. She stands outside and looks up at the sky when the wind blows.

Blackie "sings" when she is happy. She sits on my lap, flips over onto her back, and sings while I scratch her belly. If I sing to her, she sings along. Her singing gets louder and louder, until the other dogs try to hide from the noise.

Blackie has a bedtime ritual. She is the only dog who refuses to use the doggie steps to climb up on the bed. Blackie jumps up on one side of the bed, walks across both of us, and settles into her favorite spot on the opposite side of the bed. She doesn't stay there long. After about half an hour, she jumps off the bed and sleeps in the bathroom.

Blackie loves to hide in closets. She has been trapped in a closet too many times to count. After several frantic searches for her, we have learned to check the closets first. She is very sneaky, so we never see her go into the closet.

On a morning walk, Blackie managed to grab a baby rabbit without me noticing. When we got home, I saw something in her mouth. I realized it was a tiny baby rabbit, still alive and squeaking. Blackie refused to let go of it. She has very strong jaws, and you cannot take anything away from her.

I took Blackie in the house, thinking she would drop the rabbit. She ran through the house and out the dog door into the back yard. I was chasing her and yelling. The commotion woke up our old dog, Barkley. He jumped out of the chair where he had been asleep and joined in the chase. Blackie finally got bored with the rabbit and dropped it in the back yard, but it was too late to save the rabbit.

After a few months, Blackie was still living with us. We had become quite attached to this crazy puppy, so we decided to adopt her. Blackie was our first "foster failure."

Blackie was very submissive as a puppy. After our two older male cockers, Bubba and Barkley, passed away, Blackie suddenly seemed to realize that she had been at our house longer than the other dogs. She quickly became the alpha dog of our pack. Blackie still growls at any dog that gets in her space. She can appear to be asleep, but if another dog walks past her, Blackie lets out a warning growl.

Blackie is very attached to her family. We take her along when we go on long walks in different locations. Blackie whines if one of us gets out of her sight. She has a terrible fear of being abandoned again.

Since Blackie became an adult, she is not as playful or destructive as she once was. She gets very playful when it is time to walk or eat. She will grab a toy from the toy box and run around the house, growling and trying to get someone to chase her. The other dogs have their leashes on, patiently waiting for their walk. Blackie runs around the house, growling at the toy like a crazy dog. When she decides she is done playing, Blackie suddenly drops the toy and walks over to get her leash put on.

Blackie's favorite toy is a large ball that is the size of a soccer ball. Blackie chases the ball around the house. She head-butts the ball and knocks things off of shelves in her craziness.

Blackie knows how to tell time. When she thinks it is dinner time, she starts whining. If we ignore her, the whining gets louder and louder, until we finally give in and get the food ready. As soon as Blackie is positive we are fixing her dinner, she gets a toy out and starts running around the house like a crazy dog, once again.

Blackie was definitely a puppy when we first met her. She almost doubled in size by the time she was an adult. She loves to steal food and treats from other dogs, and we have to constantly watch her, so she doesn't consume too many calories. We eventually had to put Blackie on a diet.

Blackie definitely does things on her own schedule. She is very strong-willed. She seems to think she is a human, not a dog.

***

BLACKIE'S WALKING ADVENTURES

As I already mentioned, we are members of a walking club, The American Volkssport Association (AVA). We have completed 10-kilometer walks all over the state and the country. Most of our dogs have accompanied us on volkswalks at one time or another. Some of the dogs enjoy it more than others. Brittany and Barkley completed hundreds of volkswalks with us.

Blackie accompanies us on most of the volkswalks we do. Blackie completed her first volkswalk in Bradford, Ohio. Her volkssporting career began the first week she lived with us.

On one of Blackie's first walks, she encountered a large bronze statue of a lion along the trail. Blackie was afraid of the statue and growled at it. She must have thought it was a big dog.

Everyone who completes a walk gets an event stamp in their record book. Each of our cockers has their own Canine Event Book. Blackie has already filled six books with event stamps.

Blackie gets very excited when we are getting ready to go for a walk. Since this is the only time she wears her harness, she knows what is happening when we get the harness out. Blackie has her own, special, bone-shaped pillow in the car. She likes to nap on the way to a walk, so she has plenty of energy to walk 10 kilometers (about six miles).

Blackie gets so excited when we arrive at the starting point that she makes "happy noises." Everyone at the start table knows she is coming because they hear Blackie before they see her. Blackie waits, very impatiently, while we register for the event.

Blackie calms down after the first kilometer or so of the walk. She walks at a steady pace. If it is warm out, Blackie likes to lie down in the shade to cool off along the trail. Checkpoints are very exciting, too. Blackie knows she will be getting a drink and possibly a treat. Blackie does not like "community" water bowls, so she can sometimes be seen drinking water out of a paper cup at a checkpoint.

Blackie loves to walk with her Aunt Thelma. Blackie's most important job is pulling Thelma up the hills. Sometimes, Blackie gets confused and tries to pull Thelma down the hills at a fast pace.

When we stop to use the restroom along the trail, Blackie whines the entire time and stares at the restroom door until we come out. Blackie walks with us so much that a lot of people know her by name.

Sometimes we stop for a picnic lunch after a walk. Blackie usually takes a nap under the picnic table. She also likes to sleep in the car on the way home from a walk.

Blackie has completed walks in Ohio and Indiana. Some of her favorite walks are those associated with festivals. Blackie loves popcorn, and many of the festival walks have popcorn for sale. Blackie knows we will buy some popcorn to share with her after the walk.

Blackie also loves walking in parks. She is fascinated by rabbits and squirrels. If she was not kept on a leash, she would probably chase the wild animals all over the park.

BLONDIE, THE PUPPY MILL MOM

Blondie spent the first three years of her life in a puppy mill. She gave birth to three litters of puppies in less than three years. Something went very wrong during her third birthing experience, so her owners dumped Blondie at the Clark County (Ohio) Humane Society. Blondie was fortunate to be rescued by the wonderful people at Columbus Cocker Rescue. Blondie was a small, buff cocker spaniel. She only weighed 18 pounds.

Randy saw Blondie's photo online. He thought she looked like a miniature version of our first cocker spaniel, Brittany, who had passed away a few months earlier. I was not ready for another dog.

We ended up bringing Blackie and Blondie home on the same weekend. I did not realize Randy was looking at Blondie online. He did not realize I was thinking about fostering Blackie. So we ended up with two young female cockers.

Blondie came to our home on a trial visit. We soon noticed that she was not feeling well. She had a bladder infection that she was already taking medication for, along with a bad cold and nasal discharge.

We took Blondie to our vet for a check-up. He said Blondie was a very sick little girl. He was not sure if she had the dog flu or just a bad virus. He gave her a shot and more medication. He recommended Blondie be quarantined for two weeks. We reluctantly returned Blondie to her foster mom. She was very sad to leave her new family after only four days. She really had fun living at our house. She had lots of toys to play with. Blondie loved her new playmate, Blackie, our foster puppy.

After about two weeks, Blondie was feeling better. Her foster mom did not want to give her up again, as she had fallen in love with Blondie. After much discussion, she allowed Blondie to return to our home. Blondie was very excited the day we went to get her and give her a second chance. We were so happy to have her back that the first thing we did was to take Blondie to the pet store and let her pick out a new toy. She tried to show us how happy she was by jumping up and biting us on the leg. Blondie was so excited to be home and to see Blackie and all of their toys. She was still not healthy. She had to take medication for three more weeks.

The rescue had named her "Fiona." We soon discovered it was because, just like the character in the movie *Shrek*, she seemed to have two personalities. The Fiona in the movie changed at night. This dog changed whenever she went outside of our house. She was the best little dog inside the house. Outside was quite a different story.

We decided to name her Blondie Fiona. The name fits her well. She is the typical blonde stereotype people love to joke about. Blondie causes us to shake our heads and laugh many times when she acts like a "dumb blonde."

Blondie had many issues after living in a crate for three years. She did not know how to be part of a loving family. Of course, she did not want to be put into a crate. Her first night back at our home, she destroyed her crate. Fortunately, we checked on her frequently. She had her head stuck between the door and the side of the crate and was having trouble breathing.

After that, Blondie got a new plastic crate. She managed to destroy it, too. She now has a special, reinforced crate that we refer to as "Ft. Knox," but she still chews up every blanket we put in it. When we put her outside, she chewed on the door, trying to get back inside with us. She finally had a loving family and did not want us out of her sight.

Blondie destroyed anything she could find when we left her alone. She chewed up several water bowls, clothing, shoes, and a picture frame. If we went outside to get the mail, Blondie got mad because we left her, so she found something to destroy. I started carrying Blondie out to the mailbox with me.

One cool autumn day, we left Blondie in the car after we took her on a six-mile walk. While we had lunch with a friend, Blondie destroyed the door panel of the car. She even chewed on the shoulder harness. The vet gave Blondie some medication to calm her down.

Blondie is missing most of her teeth because of her chewing habit. Most of the time her tongue hangs out of her mouth because of the missing teeth. Blondie has had a few health issues: a hernia, a bad knee, and a heart murmur. None of the issues have slowed her down at all.

Blondie did not know how to walk on a leash. She would get so excited to go for a walk that she pulled as hard as she could until her paws bled. Blondie's paws were very sensitive since she was never taken outside for the first three years of her life. She did not like walking in leaves since she had never done it before. Blondie did not like the feel of snow and ice on her paws and refused to go outside. The first winter Blondie lived at our house, we had to carry her outside, so she could do her business.

Now, Blondie loves to run and play in the snow. When we are walking, she gets so excited that she whines and barks non-stop. We have to constantly remind her that she needs to walk quietly. Whenever she sees a person outside, Blondie wants to go see them because she is sure they want to pet her.

Blondie loves everyone, except cats. On one of our walks, a cat attacked her. The cat tried to scratch her face, and one of the cat's claws became stuck in Blondie's cheek. We had to hit the cat with a stick to make it leave her alone.

Blondie had never been housebroken, so she didn't know she was supposed to go outside to do her business. She frequently pottied inside the house. Blondie finally learned to go outside, and she has few accidents in the house now. Blondie was very nervous at first. She sometimes had to get up several times during the night to go outside. It took many months before she was able to sleep through an entire night.

At first, Blondie wanted to eat three times a day. Now she only eats once a day, but she cleans her bowl in less than two minutes. She is not aggressive with food or toys. Blondie will let us take things from her. She never growls at anyone, except Blackie when they are playing tug-of-war.

Blondie loves tennis balls. She constantly has one in her mouth. As soon as she is let out of her crate, Blondie goes to the toy box to find a tennis ball. She usually takes a tennis ball to bed with her. Blondie prefers to sleep on an old bed pillow, probably because it has our scent on it. She sleeps on the floor beside our bed. In the middle of the night, she climbs up on the bed and walks across us. She curls up on our pillow, as close to us as she can get.

Although it has been a long time since she had puppies, Blondie still thinks she is everyone's mother. She tries to lick the other dogs as if they are her puppies. Her evening ritual is to lick Randy's arms. She will not quit until she is satisfied that she has done her duty.

Blondie was diagnosed with a heart murmur around the age of five. It really didn't cause her any problems, at first. At age eight, Blondie began to cough, so we made a visit to the vet. He diagnosed Blondie with high blood pressure and a leaky heart valve. Our vet did not really give us much hope for Blondie. He explained several scenarios that could take place as the heart disease progressed.

Not ready to give up on Blondie, we found a vet who specialized in internal medicine. We took Blondie there after getting a referral from our regular vet. An ultrasound revealed that she had not one, but two leaky valves. Blondie was given four different medications. The medications improved Blondie's quality of life. She has check-ups with the specialist every six months.

The following week, we took the cockers to a Halloween party at a private dog park. They all ran to the pond, waded a little, got a drink, and got out of the water. A few minutes later, Blondie jumped into the pond and started swimming across. I frantically called for her to come back to me. I was about ready to jump in and get her. I had a camera in my hand, but I was too worried to take her picture.

Blondie dog paddled all the way across the pond, got out, shook off the water, and ran after the other dogs. I spent the next half-hour explaining to everyone why Blondie was so wet.

After lunch, the dogs played a Halloween game - bobbing for rubber ducks in a bucket of water. Blondie was the star of the game. She grabbed the ducks, one after another. We decided Blondie was a water lover, after all.

Blondie still goes like the "Energizer Bunny," but she no longer has enough energy to climb over the baby gates we use to keep the dogs out of certain parts of our house.

Blondie has come a long way since she joined our family. We hired a personal trainer to work with Blondie for several months. We soon noticed a big improvement in her behavior.

It is not Blondie's fault that she lived in a puppy mill for three years and never learned how to be a family pet. She was only a breeding machine. It is possible for a puppy mill mother to become a happy family pet. It takes lots of love and patience. It takes time to overcome all of the bad habits she learned in the first years of her "existence." We can't call it "life," as it isn't much of a life for a dog.

***

BLONDIE'S PUPPY MILL FACTS

- Puppy mills are one of America's most shameful secrets. Puppy mills are the hidden world of substandard kennels where dogs are caged like chickens and forced to produce puppies over and over, until they can produce no more.

- A rescued puppy mill dog may suffer tremendous separation anxiety and become destructive when the owner leaves.

- Breeders get rid of older female dogs when they become worn out from having so many litters so close together.

- Dogs frequently emerge from puppy mills in shockingly bad shape. Some of the dogs have mange, bladder stones, multiple tumors, and broken jaws or backs.

- Puppy mill dogs are frightened and malnourished. They are rarely given medical attention of any kind; they shiver in the cold days of winter and bake in the summer heat. These dogs never know kindness or the slightest affection. They are prisoners for profit.

- Dogs rescued from puppy mills have never lived indoors. They are often difficult to housetrain. These dogs lack socialization and often have a fear of ordinary noises and activities.

- Puppy millers wean puppies too early, which instills a permanent sense of fearfulness and insecurity.

- The puppies born to these puppy mill breeding dogs are sold to unsuspecting buyers through pet shops and websites. The only way to avoid buying a dog from a puppy mill is to meet the breeder and visit the kennel personally.

- Being a breeding dog in a puppy mill is the most brutally mundane life imaginable. Breeding dogs languish for five or ten years or more in a cage before they are finally put out of their misery – often with a bullet to the head.

- Puppy mill dogs quickly learn that each new day is not something to savor, but something to endure.

- Families who rescue puppy mill survivors realize for themselves the awful truth about the dark side of breeding and begin spreading the word, one person at a time.

THE BLACK AND BLONDE TAG TEAM

Blackie and Blondie became instant friends. They found lots of mischief to get into together. We call them "The Black and Blonde Tag Team."

When we first brought the girls home, they were small enough to get under our shed, so we purchased some bags of topsoil to fill in the space. We left the bags on our patio. About an hour later, we had a huge pile of dirt on the patio. The girls had torn open every bag of soil.

One time we left them in the car while we went inside to order a pizza. When we returned five minutes later, they had eaten half a bag of buttered popcorn. The bag was on the floor of the car. Both girls were fastened in with harnesses and seatbelts, but Blondie had managed to reach the bag, open it, and share it with Blackie. Blondie's stomach looked much larger than usual, so she couldn't deny her evil deed.

Another time, I left the girls in the house while I did yard work. I went to check on them and found them both sitting next to the remains of a framed photo. They had removed the frame from an end table and managed to destroy it. They had broken the glass into pieces. It was a miracle they were not injured. They had not touched the photo in the frame, so I was able to salvage that.

Blondie acted like a puppy, since she had never been able to be a puppy at the puppy mill. She was too busy having puppies of her own. Some days I felt like I was raising twin toddlers, and I wanted to cry. Things got better when the girls outgrew the puppy stage.

***

BLACKIE AND BLONDIE'S VET ADVENTURES

The first time I took Blackie and Blondie to the vet's office for their yearly checkups and shots, it was quite an adventure. They were excited to get in the car early in the morning, expecting to go somewhere fun, like the park.

A golden retriever and two cats were also waiting to see the doctor. The golden retriever's owner was singing baby songs and making baby noises to it, which distracted Blackie and Blondie as they were trying to take a nap. I never sing lullabies to them. They just have to fall asleep by themselves. Finally, the golden retriever's owner said she couldn't wait any longer. She told the vet tech to put the golden in a crate, and her husband would pick him up later. So much for the lullabies!

Another lady came in with a spoiled little terrier. She held it on her lap and talked to it in German. She said the dog was scared because it had never been away from its sister. The terrier's owner called a friend on her cell phone and told the friend to talk to the dog to calm it down. The dog only became noisier and more excited after hearing the friend on the cell phone. I never let my dogs talk on the phone.

Suddenly the door opened, and an old man almost fell into the office. He hadn't seen the step. It scared Blackie and Blondie who thought the man was lunging at them. Blackie barked and growled at the man. He was carrying a plastic bag full of dog waste. He gave it to the lady at the desk. The girls thought that was funny, since I usually throw theirs in the garbage.

A standard poodle and a cat came in. That cat was a very loud and unhappy cat. The mailman came in next. Blackie barked at him for good measure, since she knew he was not our friendly mailman, Tommy.

A lady came in with a tiny little "Taco Bell dog" (a Chihuahua). Blackie went crazy. She knew that we like to eat Taco Bell food, so she thought maybe this little guy was a snack. Blackie barked so much that finally, one of the cat owners offered to give his chair to the Taco Bell dog's mom so that she could get away from Blackie and her barking. I told the Taco-Bell-dog lady that we had been waiting for more than an hour, and the cockers were getting bored.

The lady asked if we had an appointment, and I told her we certainly did!

The receptionist said there had been an emergency. An elderly Sheltie was getting fluid drained from his lungs. It took more than an hour to drain 1.5 gallons of fluid from the poor old boy. He finally came out and wasn't looking too happy. He was shaved and had a bag on one side of his stomach. He could hardly walk out the door.

Then, another emergency case came in. A German shepherd was brought in by his owners. They said he had been chasing a squirrel and had run into the road. He was hit by not one, but two cars. The lady jokingly said at least he didn't get hit by a semi. The vet said he would have to take some X-rays. The dog's owners blamed it all on the squirrel. I guess the squirrel should have been on a leash!

After waiting for more than an hour, they finally said Blackie and Blondie could go into the exam room. The girls got their shots and check-ups. They each got a treat from the vet's treat jar. The girls and I all needed a nap. It was a long, tiring, and expensive morning.

BETSY, A DADDY'S GIRL

*A*few weeks after losing Barkley, we were asked by Columbus Cocker Rescue to evaluate a cocker at the Montgomery County (Ohio) Animal Resource Center. The shelter is about five miles from our house, so we decided to go, even though we were still devastated about Barkley's passing.

The cocker we were supposed to evaluate had an adoption hold by the time we arrived. We were told that another cocker had recently come in. We decided to go look at it. We wouldn't have to come back another day if we checked the cocker out and took some photos while we were already there.

The lady led us to the back. We looked all around, not seeing a cocker anywhere. We saw what we thought was a black poodle. The lady pointed to the dog and said her name was Sue Bee. We took a few photos of the black fur ball. She was very small, 18 pounds, with a ton of fur. We could not even see her face. Sue Bee was the most pathetic little waif. She was bouncing all over the kennel because she was so excited to have some attention from people. It was hard to get a good picture.

Sue Bee had been wandering the streets near our house. It was a wonder that we had never seen her roaming around. The owners had moved away and left Sue Bee behind. She had just delivered a litter of puppies within the last eight weeks. Sue Bee had gotten kennel cough at the shelter.

I emailed the photos to the director of the rescue. She said Columbus Cocker Rescue would take Sue Bee if she was not adopted by the end of the week, though she knew Sue Bee might be a challenge to place. For some reason, people don't want to adopt black dogs.

I called the shelter to check on Sue Bee for the rescue. The lady said Sue Bee had an approved application and would be going to her new home later that day. I felt happy for Sue Bee and yet sad, too. I had been thinking about her a lot. Something about Sue Bee was tugging at my heart. I told the lady to let us know if the adoption did not work out because we might be interested in Sue Bee. The words seemed to slip out of my mouth before I knew what I was saying. I wasn't too worried because I was sure Sue Bee was going to be adopted.

We had been planning a vacation for the following month. We agreed we would not even think about looking for another cocker until after vacation. We had decided that our new cocker would not be black, since we already had a black female cocker. We had two females already, so it had to be a male.

An hour later, the lady called and said the adoption had fallen through. She wanted to know when we could pick up Sue Bee. I told her we would have to discuss it. Randy reminded me that I had said "no more black dogs" and "no more female dogs." Sue Bee was black and female. He also reminded me about our upcoming vacation. We didn't really need another dog to board. Randy finally told me to do whatever I wanted to do about Sue Bee, and he would go along with my decision.

The next day, I stopped by the shelter to visit Sue Bee. I took her to the outside play area. Sue Bee didn't have any interest in playing. All she wanted to do was to be held. She was starved for attention. I took some more photos.

We discussed it further and decided Sue Bee was a good fit for us. We knew that if we waited until after our vacation, Sue Bee might be adopted. We told the shelter lady that Sue Bee had just found a home.

We knew Sue Bee needed a different name. We finally decided to name her Betsy Sue, keeping part of her original name.

Betsy settled in very well. It was fall, and we had a yard full of leaves. Every time she went outside, Betsy came in with a bunch of leaves stuck in her long fur. We had to wait 10 days to get the stitches removed from her spay surgery. Then we took her to meet our vet. He thought she was adorable. He checked her over and said there was no way she was four years old, like the shelter had told us. He doubted that she was even two years old, after looking at her teeth. He said she was barely old enough to have had a litter of puppies.

The next day, we took Betsy to our groomer. I jokingly said that I thought there was a dog under all that fur. I asked the groomer to find that dog for us. I was amazed when I picked Betsy up that afternoon. She was beautiful. Her coat was very shiny, and we were surprised to discover that she has a white chest. She looked like she was wearing a tuxedo. Betsy happily posed for photos, and she seemed very proud of her new look.

Soon, it was time for our vacation. We were worried about leaving Betsy. We didn't want her to think she was being abandoned again, but she was fine at the kennel. When we got back home, Betsy settled in like she had been part of our family forever. She never had an accident in the house, and she never chewed on anything. She was very different from the other two girls, who had chewed up and destroyed half of our possessions in their first two years with us.

Betsy became very attached to Randy. She constantly wanted to sit on his lap and sleep next to him at night. If another dog tried to join her, she gave them a warning growl. Randy taught her to "high five." When he went away on business trips, Betsy would not eat while he was gone. She would sleep near the front door, waiting for him to return. I would take Betsy along to the airport to pick up Randy. She could not contain her excitement when she saw him.

Betsy has a cherry eye that only pops out occasionally (cherry eye is non-life-threatening condition where the third eyelid protrudes from the eye area as a red, fleshy mass). Betsy is very wiggly when she is excited. During one trip to the groomer, she moved at the wrong time, and the groomer cut her under the eye. Betsy had emergency surgery to repair the cut. It was the same eye that has the cherry eye. Betsy has very long eyelashes. We call them her "movie star lashes." One time, the groomer trimmed the lashes very short, and Randy was devastated.

Betsy was the first member of our family to meet our new young vet, after our beloved vet of many years retired suddenly. Betsy had a cyst on her neck that had continued to grow. One day it started seeping blood, so off to the vet's office we went. We scheduled her surgery for the following week.

When I went to pick Betsy up on the afternoon of her surgery, I asked to speak to the vet. A young man in his 20s with spiked hair walked out and greeted me. I was shocked to find out that our regular vet had been planning to retire and hadn't told anyone, not even his staff.

After I got over my initial shock and Betsy made a full recovery, I warmed up to the new vet. He had recently graduated from vet school and was up to date on the latest medicines and techniques. His young wife is also a vet, and they are practicing together now. This has resulted in shorter wait times and the ability to get a second opinion in one visit.

Betsy loves people, but she does not care much for other dogs and prefers to be alone. She sleeps under the bed during the day. She only plays with toys when no other dogs are around. She loves to lie in the sun on very hot days. Betsy also loves to roll in snow and come in the house looking like a white dog instead of a black dog.

Betsy sometimes thinks she is a cat. She likes to bat at things, like tennis balls. One of her nicknames is "Battin' Betsy." She also likes to bark if she thinks we are going outside to play with her, so we also call her "Barkin' Betsy."

BRANDON, OUR PARTI BOY

A few weeks after we lost Bubba to cancer, Randy wanted to go to "Mingle with the Mutts," a dog adoption event in Columbus, Ohio. On the way there, I kept reminding him that we were just looking and not bringing home any more dogs. We were really attached to Bubba, since we had him for 12 years. Once again, I said, "No more dogs."

Randy spotted a young chocolate-and-white parti cocker spaniel male named Dandy. He kept looking at this dog, and

I could tell he was in love. Finally, we decided to bring Dandy home for a trial visit. We were pre-approved, since we had already adopted Blondie from Columbus Cocker Rescue. We were also rescue volunteers.

Dandy was an owner surrender, along with his father, Fudge. The family had lost their home in an early spring flood along the Ohio River. Dandy had just been released for adoption. He was being treated for parvo when he came into rescue. He was very ill, and it was not certain he would survive. When we met him, Dandy had just been given a clean bill of health.

We had our vet check Dandy over right away. He could find no evidence of parvo and thought it was only a false positive. Dandy was a great dog, and he soon became a part of our family. We renamed him Brandon.

Brandon's full name is Brandon Emil Phillips Adams. He is named for my favorite Cincinnati Reds baseball player, Brandon Phillips. When I am watching a Reds game on television and cheering for Brandon the second baseman, Brandon the dog has learned to ignore me.

Brandon was one year old when we adopted him, and we were told that he was fully grown. Evidently, no one told Brandon that he was fully grown because he just kept growing!

Brandon was very thin when we first adopted him, probably because he had been so sick. I nicknamed him "Noodle" because he would stretch out on the floor and scoot around on his belly. He reminded me of a noodle. Later, when Brandon began to fill out, I told him I would have to change his nickname to "Macaroni." By then, he thought his name was Noodle.

Brandon still had a lot of puppy energy. Blackie was the only one of our cockers who would play with him. Brandon loved to play tug-of-war with Blackie. After a while, Blackie would tire of the game and retreat to a corner so she could destroy the rope toy.

We soon learned that Brandon had a hobby of collecting things. He would find a "treasure" in the house and take it outside to destroy it. Brandon is especially fond of shiny objects, like nail clippers. He has destroyed pencils, a telephone cord, and dozens of toys. He always does his evil deeds in the same spot in our yard. If something is missing, we go check Brandon's special place. If Brandon is caught in the act of stealing something, he will bolt out the dog door and run around the yard. He can run very fast. Brandon loves to be chased because he knows no one can catch him!

Brandon also likes to collect things from outside, like rocks, sticks, leaves, and nuts. He brings his outside treasures into the house and deposits them proudly on the carpet.

Brandon loves to bark at squirrels in our trees. He does it during the day and sometimes in the middle of the night. I often wake up from a sound sleep, hear a barking dog, and realize it is Brandon.

Brandon is terrified of anything new - people, objects, noises. Brandon will run outside and hide if we have house guests (even people he has previously met). He hides if we get a new piece of furniture or a new appliance.

One winter we had a substitute dog sitter at our house. Brandon was fine the first time. The second (and last) time, Brandon could not be coaxed back inside. When the sitter called, I told her how to trick Brandon to come back inside. We didn't receive any more phone calls, so we assumed Brandon had come inside.

When we pulled into the driveway, we heard Brandon barking by the gate. He had stayed outside the entire afternoon. The other dogs were in their crates, and Brandon's treat was still lying on the floor in front of his crate. Brandon was very cold, since it was the middle of winter, with temperatures in the single digits.

We later found out the dog sitter had brought her son along, after we had told her not to. Brandon is terrified of most men. Since Brandon had never met the son, there was no way he was going back inside the house - not even to grab his treat.

We did not put up our Christmas tree for several years due to Brandon's habit of stealing things. When Brandon was five, I decided that he had grown up enough to leave the tree alone. As I was decorating the tree, I noticed Brandon stealing an ornament out of the box.

After the tree was decorated, Brandon would sit and stare at it. He would walk around the room, trying to figure out how to get close to it, since it was wedged into a corner that was not easily accessible to the dogs. Brandon seemed to be fascinated by the Christmas tree. He never even tried to hide from it.

Brandon had a bad experience when we took him to a grooming school. We never really found out what happened to him. I was told several different versions of the story. Brandon had a quarter-sized wound on his side that required several staples.

While the wound healed, Brandon had to wear an E-collar, and he was terrified. He was shaking and running into the walls. We put him in the car and drove to the pet store to buy him an inflatable "donut" collar. He was much happier after that. We never took him, or any of our cockers, to the grooming school again after that bad experience.

Brandon is the king at our house. He has lived with six female cockers but never another male. Our friend Thelma jokes about "King Brandon and his harem." We joke that he must think he's a girl, since he has never once lifted his leg.

After we adopted Brandon, some of my friends told me that parti cockers are wild and like to party. I had never heard that before, but it is certainly true of Brandon.

Brandon has very long legs and large paws. We are often asked if he is a springer spaniel. We believe he may have some springer blood in him, although our vet does not agree. We saw a dog at the vet's office one day who looked just like a smaller Brandon. That dog's name was Jerry Springer!

BEEZUS, THE SQUIRREL HUNTER

*I*n the fall of the same year we adopted Brandon, we went to the dog adoption event again. Our friends Bob and Alice had adopted a cocker spaniel named Cruiser from Columbus Cocker Rescue. They were looking for a second cocker. Bob asked us to go with them to help pick out a dog. They ended up adopting Sasha (a miniature of Brandon) that day.

Randy and I love red cocker spaniels and were still missing Bubba, our old red boy, when we walked into the Cocker Rescue tent and saw the most beautiful red female cocker. Randy was drawn to her like a magnet. He was soon walking around the parking lot with Honey Bee.

At the end of the event, Randy asked the rescue director if we could take Honey Bee home with us as a foster dog for a few weeks. I knew what he had in mind! By the next morning, I knew Honey Bee was not leaving.

We renamed her Beezus. We had used so many "B" names for our previous cockers that we were having trouble finding a name we could agree on. Beezus was a character in the *Beezus and Ramona* book series by Beverly Cleary. I had read the books as a child. One of the books had recently been made into a movie, *Ramona and Beezus*. It seems like I am the only person who ever read those books, since I am constantly explaining the origin of Beezus' name to people.

Beezus is actually a "docker" - part cocker spaniel and part dachshund. She has a long body and a long snout. With her ears shaved close, she looks like a dachshund. We let her ears grow out, so she looks more like a cocker.

Brandon and Beezus became best friends very quickly, maybe because they are close to the same age. Brandon and Beezus play very rough, rolling around on the floor and growling at each other. At first, we thought someone was going to get hurt. We quickly realized it is just how they play. They have never hurt each other.

Brandon and Beezus will playfully bite each other on the mouth and neck. I was told that is the ultimate sign of affection between two dogs.

When one of the pair is at the groomer or vet's office, the other one is lost and wanders around the house aimlessly. We can't take Brandon and Beezus to the groomer on the same day. They get too wild when they are together. As the groomer explained to us, "They feed off each other."

Beezus loves to hunt. She brought a big, dead bird into the house and hid it behind the couch. When I noticed she was spending a lot of time behind the couch, I decided to investigate and found her treasure, which was starting to smell bad.

Another time, Beezus brought a dead bird into the house and dropped it on the carpet. I didn't notice the bird, until Randy picked it up by the leg and asked if I was saving it for something.

Beezus also loves to stalk squirrels and even tries to climb trees to get them. She has jumped up on our privacy fence a few times. I was worried that she was going to climb over the fence.

Beezus did catch a squirrel when she was almost five years old. A squirrel was sitting near the sidewalk one morning on our walk. I was sure the squirrel would run when it saw three cocker spaniels, so we kept walking. The squirrel did run – right across the sidewalk in front of us. At first, I did not realize Beezus had grabbed it, since she had not even jerked on the leash.

Beezus was on a coupler with Brandon, so catching the squirrel was no easy feat. Beezus had a hold on the squirrel's stomach. The squirrel was flailing and squeaking. I told Beezus to "drop it," and she did, after I repeated the command several times. The squirrel ran under a large pine tree. The cockers tried to chase it, and I almost fell head-first into the pine tree.

After the squirrel incident, I started telling the cockers to "walk, don't stalk." Even a year later, they look for a squirrel in that tree every morning.

A few months after the squirrel incident, I saw Beezus guarding something near a tree in our back yard. At first, I thought it was a kitten. Then, I realized it was actually a dead baby squirrel with the tail missing. Beezus was not happy when I took her treasure away.

Beezus will sit by the dog door and watch for squirrels in the back yard for hours at a time. We can't even say the word "squirrel" around Beezus, so we now refer to those pesky creatures as "SQs."

We took the cockers to get their photo taken with Santa Claus at the pet store. A family with three kids and three ferrets was in line behind us. One of the kids let one of the ferrets out of the cage and carried it over near the cockers. Beezus noticed it right away, so I quickly walked her down another aisle to avert a potential tragedy for the ferret.

I went to pick Beezus up at the vet's office after she got her teeth cleaned one day. A young girl was walking around the office holding a guinea pig. I was getting worried because I knew how much Beezus likes to stalk small animals. Beezus was still groggy from the anesthetic, so the guinea pig was safe.

Beezus loves to dig holes in our yard. She digs up rocks and tree roots. She digs new holes as fast as we can fill in the old ones. By the end of summer, our yard is full of fenced-off areas where holes have been filled. Beezus knows she is not supposed to dig. She always gets a time out in her crate, followed by a bath, which she hates. Yet she continues to dig holes. Beezus' nickname is "Digger."

BUFFIE,
OUR OLD PRINCESS

Didi was a buff-and-white cocker spaniel. She was abandoned on a Columbus, Ohio, street in the middle of a cold, snowy January. She ended up at the Franklin County Humane Society. The shelter was not going to put Didi up for adoption, since she was 12 years old. Her only hope was a rescue group.

Didi had been found with another cocker, a six-year-old male named Dante. Dante had an eye infection and ended up losing an eye. Columbus Cocker Rescue accepted both Didi and Dante.

We were asked to foster Didi. We soon decided to be her permanent foster family. She would live out the rest of her life with our family. The rescue would be responsible for her vet bills. We just had to feed her, groom her, and love her.

Didi had badly infected ears. We soon discovered she was deaf, probably due to the untreated ear infections. She also had luxating patellas and early stage kidney failure. She spent a lot of time drinking and going potty.

We decided to rename her Buffie. Since she was deaf, she had no idea what we called her, anyhow.

On the long car ride to our house, Buffie kissed me constantly. She never gave me any kisses after that first night. For about two months, Buffie wanted to sit on my lap every evening. I would chase the other dogs away so that Buffie could have her special bonding time.

After a few months, Buffie did not want to sit on my lap anymore. It seemed as if she finally felt safe and secure in her new home. She was happy to sleep on her dog bed. Whenever she would wake up, Buffie would look around the room to see where I was, then lay her head down and continue her nap.

Buffie could be sound asleep, and when I left the room, she would immediately wake up and start looking for me. She did the same thing when I left the house.

Buffie fit into our family of cockers like she had always been there. Our dogs seem to be very accepting of older cockers. We'd previously had an older male foster cocker named Rodger. Our dogs know that the older cockers aren't going to play with them and just want to be left alone.

Brandon did try to get Buffie to play with him. He finally gave up because I constantly reminded him that Buffie was old enough to be his great-grandmother!

Buffie learned American Sign Language. I was the one who taught her to respond to the signs. At bedtime, Randy would give her the sign for "go out." Buffie would immediately look at me. As soon as I gave her the sign for "go out," she would go outside.

Buffie was usually cold, even in the summer months. She had a large wardrobe of colorful sweaters. She was rarely seen "naked" (without a sweater). Buffie had arthritis, which caused her to shake uncontrollably, even when it was 90 degrees outside.

Buffie's favorite color was pink. She had a complete set of pink accessories. When we took her to Gahanna Animal Hospital in Columbus, the vet remarked that Buffie was "all pinked out."

Buffie had limited vision. She often stepped in the water bowl. She would stare at the bowl for several minutes before drinking, as if she couldn't see the water. We tried a variety of different water bowls for her. Buffie also had problems seeing her food, so we experimented with different colors of bowls. We finally found a color that worked well for her.

Buffie often got under our bed at night. Sometimes only her head was visible. I have never figured out how she managed to get under the bed since she had mobility issues. She always managed to get out without assistance.

Buffie walked around the house at her slow, steady pace. She fell down a lot, especially on wet or slippery surfaces. She couldn't walk on wet or icy sidewalks. If another dog bumped into her, Buffie would fall down. She often fell up the curbs. Later, the curbs in our neighborhood were made handicap accessible, but Buffie's walking days were over by then.

When I had knee surgery and was using a walker, I felt as old as Buffie. One day, I sensed someone beside me. I looked down, and Buffie walked right through my walker, as if I was in her way. I was walking too slowly for her.

Buffie loved to walk with us. She held her head up high and pranced along like the princess she had become since she adopted us. I am not sure what the first 12 years of Buffie's life were like. She must have been someone's beloved pet.

All I know is Buffie lived out the remaining days of her life like royalty!

BROWNIE,
A CHOCOLATE DELIGHT

KoKoa was a chocolate cocker spaniel. She was abandoned by her owners at the Clark County (Ohio) Humane Society when she was six years old. The only family she had ever known could no longer care for her.

KoKoa was soon rescued by Columbus Cocker Rescue. The rescue was overflowing with cockers at the time, so KoKoa was placed in boarding at Camp Bow Wow. About a week after KoKoa's arrival at the Camp, we agreed to foster her. We picked her up at the Camp and took her home.

KoKoa was very thin. She only weighed 19 pounds. She had an ear infection, some skin issues, and several bald spots on her neck and her behind. She had an old scar on her nose, probably from being hit with something.

We took KoKoa to an adoption event. A family was interested in her but concerned that she was "too old." The man was checking her teeth in a way that reminded me of someone kicking the tires on a used car they were looking at. The family decided on a younger cocker instead.

After a few months and no potential adopters in sight, we decided to make KoKoa a permanent member of our dog pack. She got along very well with our other six cockers. They all accepted her, and she respected the "pack order." The rescue director told us to just "keep her." We made it official by filling out an adoption application and making a donation to the rescue.

The next day, KoKoa had a seizure. It was a mild one, and she recovered in a matter of minutes.

We decided to change her name to Brownie. At the time, I had been baking brownies every day. Randy took them to work and sold them to his co-workers to raise money for the rescue.

After about six months, Brownie started to come out of her shell. She became very playful and tried to get the other dogs to play with her. She seemed to know which dogs might play with her and which ones wanted to be left alone. Brownie started playing with toys and carrying them around the house with her. She especially liked to destroy tennis balls.

Brownie seemed to love food and treats. She would grab the treat out of my hand, often nipping my fingers accidentally in her excitement. Brownie ate her food very fast, as if someone was going to take it away from her. After about a year, Brownie began to eat her food at a slower, more relaxed pace. She realized no one was going to take her food away before she was finished.

Brownie showed signs that she had been abused at her previous home. She would flinch every time someone reached out a hand to pet her. For many months, I would pat her on the head every time I walked past her. Brownie finally realized that not all hands were going to hurt her. She started giving us kisses after living with our family for more than a year.

Brownie was also afraid of feet. Any time someone's foot got too close to her, she would run off. Apparently, she had also been kicked at her previous home.

A year after her first seizure, Brownie had a more serious seizure. She spent the entire long holiday weekend trying to hide. She wanted to stay outside during the day. At night, I coaxed her into the house, and she ran under the bed. She refused to come out, so I slid her dinner under the bed, and she ate some of it.

I took Brownie to the vet the following week. He didn't think it was a seizure. He did a series of tests and ruled out everything else, so he decided it was a seizure. After that episode, Brownie became even more loving and gave us kisses more frequently.

Brownie has her favorite dog bed. Every night, she watches for signs that we are getting ready to go to bed. Brownie runs to the bedroom and claims her favorite bed before another dog does. Every new foster dog since Brownie has wanted that same dog bed.

When Brownie got older, she became incontinent. Her favorite bed was wet every morning. The vet did several tests and determined that Brownie had "old age incontinence," even though she was only eight years old. The vet prescribed some medication that quickly took care of the problem. No more wet beds!

BRAGGS, FROM RAGS TO RICHES

fter we made the decision to only foster older dogs, we were told that the rescue had the "perfect" foster dog for us. Rags had been in boarding for more than a month, since she had some health issues and couldn't be in a foster home at first. We thought it over for about a week and finally decided to foster Rags.

We drove to Columbus one evening to pick up Rags. We were surprised when we saw her. Rags looked like she had been very appropriately named. She looked like a pathetic waif. When we got on the interstate to return to our home, Rags sat up in the back seat and let out a loud howl. It surprised us, and at first we thought maybe something was wrong with her.

Rags was a nine-year-old, red-and-white cocker spaniel. She had been found roaming the streets as a stray and ended up at the Franklin County (Ohio) Humane Society. Rags had somehow become covered with oil and had to be given six baths to get rid of most of the oil. She had severe skin issues. Her little rear had no fur, and the skin had become as tough as leather. Rags had water-filled blisters on her feet and legs.

I thought Rags was the saddest-looking cocker I had ever seen. She certainly was not very attractive. She had very droopy, sad eyes. The fur around her eyes was gone, which made her look even sadder. We were told many times in the next few months that Rags looked very sad.

Rags had to be bathed with medicated shampoo three times a week. She had to soak in the bathtub for 10 minutes each time. Rags had several medications to help with the itching, and we started giving her vitamins to help with her skin problems. After a few months, the medicated baths decreased to twice weekly and then once a week. Rags also had ear infections, so she needed to have her ears cleaned frequently.

After about three months, Rags was given a good report by the rescue's vet. She no longer needed the medication or the baths. Her fur was slowly growing back. Eventually, the fur around her eyes and on her rear grew back, much to our surprise.

We entered Rags' photo in a Fourth of July patriotic photo contest at a pet store, and she won third place out of hundreds of entries. She donated her prize, a $50 pet store gift card, to Columbus Cocker Rescue.

Rags became more energetic and playful when she started feeling better and wasn't spending a good portion of her day itching and scratching. She began to get toys out of the toy box. Her favorite toys are Nylabones. Every evening, she carefully selects one from the toy box and chews on it for about half an hour. As a result, she has very good-looking teeth for her age.

Rags quickly became attached to us. She follows me around the house and sometimes wraps her paws around my ankle. Rags claimed Brownie's favorite dog bed as her own, so we had to buy a special bed just for Rags. Eventually, she decided she would rather sleep on our bed with most of the other dogs.

Rags does not like to be crated and will howl loudly when she is confined. She would scoot her crate across the floor, so we had to wedge a board in front of it to keep her crate in place. Rags likes to hide when it is crate-time.

Rags also likes to scratch on doors and walls if we get out of her sight. She knocks the baby gates over if we go outside to get the mail. She has a terrible fear of being abandoned again.

We took Rags to see Santa for the first time at age 10. She was not very happy to sit on Santa's lap and have her picture taken. She was shaking like a leaf, but Santa did get a nice sloppy kiss from her.

We took Rags to many adoption events. Everyone commented on her beauty and her soulful face. As soon as they learned her age, they would move on to look at much younger dogs.

Rags started to hate the adoption events. She had become very attached to us. She did not like other dogs getting in her face, and she got very stressed out at these events.

After fostering her for more than a year with very little interest from potential adopters, we decided to adopt Rags. We made it official at the "Mars Adoption on the Lawn" event. This event is held at the Mars Pet Care Facility in Columbus, Ohio, every September. It is a great place to adopt a pet. Mars pays a portion of the adoption fee and supplies the adoptive family with plenty of food and treats.

Rags was also given a gift card to a local pet store. She had her official adoption photo taken with us at the Mars Event. Rags got her "15 minutes of fame" that day.

Everyone was asking what we were going to name our newest family member. Since she had been "Rags" for so long, we wanted a similar name that would not confuse her or us. In keeping with our "B" theme, we decided on "Braggs." We felt that she had plenty to brag about. Braggs has come a long way since the day she was found as a stray, covered with oil. She has gone from "rags" to "riches."

RODGER, A PERFECT GENTLEMAN

*O*ur son once said that any cocker who got its paws inside our house never left. That was not always the case. Rodger was surrendered to the Defiance County Humane Society when his elderly owner moved to an assisted living facility. Rodger was 10 years old and remained at the shelter for a few months.

Louie, one of the volunteers, often took Rodger home with him on weekends. Later that summer, the shelter asked Columbus Cocker Rescue to find a forever home for Rodger.

We happened to be going to Defiance anyway, since that is my hometown and I have family there, so we picked Rodger up at the shelter.

Rodger was reluctant to leave Louie that day, and he kept looking back at his friend. Louie's heart broke when he saw how sad Rodger was, and he knew the cocker needed to be with him permanently. He didn't say anything to us as we put Rodger in our car and drove away. Rodger was very nervous on the three-hour trip to our house, and we had to stop halfway so he could go potty.

Our cockers accepted Rodger right away and followed him around the house. A few hours after we got Rodger settled in at our house, the rescue director called to tell us Louie wanted to adopt Rodger and was willing to pick him up at our house.

I drove Rodger back to Louie's house in Defiance four days later, since I was going there anyway. Louie later realized that Rodger chose him that day.

Rodger was a very handsome, slightly overweight, black cocker. He had a very distinguished-looking white muzzle. Rodger reminded us of a black version of our Bubba. I took Rodger on a few walks around the block, and he grew tired very quickly. I don't think he was used to walking.

Louie located Rodger's former owner at the assisted living facility and took Rodger to visit many times. Rodger's former owner had dementia. After a while, he did not know Rodger, but the dog always knew his previous owner.

Rodger lived a good, long life. He was very happy and loved. Rodger was always the perfect gentleman, and he was treated like a king at Louie's house.

GOLDIE, THE DIVA

Goldie was a five-year-old cocker spaniel with a beautiful, golden, curly coat. Her first owner had passed away. No one in the family wanted Goldie or her fur sibling, Rascal, so they ended up at the shelter. Columbus Cocker Rescue took the pair in. Rascal, being the more outgoing of the two, was quickly adopted. Our friend Susan fostered Goldie.

A few months later, Susan was moving and could not keep as many dogs as she currently had. We went to a Valentine's

Day adoption event in Columbus and met Goldie. We were not planning on fostering at that time, but Susan asked if we could foster one of her two foster cockers.

Goldie did not seem to like us at first. She was very attached to Susan. Goldie warmed up to us quickly after we took her home. Since she was young and playful, Goldie did not get along with most of our pack. There were frequent fights, always involving food or treats. We quickly learned how to avoid most of the fights.

Goldie tried to attack our TV several times. If there was a dog on TV, and she heard it barking, she would run to the TV and try to get the dog. We had just gotten a new flat-screen TV, so I really didn't want her to ruin it. One morning, in an attempt to get a dog on TV, Goldie knocked the toy box over, and two dozen tennis balls went rolling everywhere.

One evening we were watching a dog movie, and Goldie tried to attack the TV a couple of times. The dog on TV was not even making any noise, but Goldie went crazy. It was like she could "see" the dog on the screen. We finally had to put her on a leash. Goldie lay on the couch, staring intently at the TV and acting sad because she couldn't get the dog.

None of our other cockers have ever acted this way. They usually just run outside, barking and looking for the dog on TV.

Goldie liked to stand up on our windowsill to look outside, and she liked to nap on my computer chair or on top of the dining room table. She was a bundle of energy. She loved to walk, but she was afraid of everyone. She was also afraid of trucks and vans, and she barked at them.

Goldie kept things lively at our house, since we always had to be alert to avoid fights. We were in love with Goldie, but she sure wreaked havoc on our family at times. We soon realized that Goldie would be happier as an only dog.

At adoption events, Goldie stayed right beside us. She only ventured away to greet a couple of the volunteers she had met before. Goldie would sometimes move away from us and check out the other dogs.

Goldie hated riding in the car. She would look out the window and then get down on the floorboard, even though she had a car harness on. She would shake like a leaf for the entire trip, probably because every time she got into a car, she seemed to end up in a new situation.

A retired lady and her teenage daughter fell in love with Goldie's photo on the rescue's website, and they wanted to meet her. We took Goldie to an adoption event where she met her new family. Goldie didn't want to leave us, just like she had not wanted to leave Susan a few months earlier. The mother and daughter looked at all the other cockers, numbering about two dozen, but they liked Goldie the best. When they left, Goldie was sitting on the daughter's lap in the car. That was progress, since she hated car rides. We sent her home with a goodie bag filled with treats, toys, bandanas, and a brush.

Goldie was with us for 50 days, so we were getting attached to her. We had known that she was only going to be a foster dog, so we had tried not to get too attached. Hopefully, we helped her to transition to her *fur*ever home. We tried to socialize Goldie by walking her a lot. We taught her to eat on her own, without someone sitting next to her and hand-feeding her. We taught Goldie to "sit," and we convinced her to stop begging at the table.

Goldie soon adjusted to her new home and her *fur*ever family. She followed her new mom around the house. Goldie got to go for walks in the park almost every day. She slept with the teenage daughter and helped her with homework.

Goldie was very loved and pampered. It seemed to be a match made in heaven. Many people commented on how beautiful Goldie was. Her new family called her "The Diva."

THE ADAMS COCKER SPANIEL FAMILY

Brittany Marie	1994 -2005
Beauford Peter "Bubba"	1994-2008
Barkley Charles	1996-2007
Buffie Lynn	1998-2010
Braggs Anne	2002 -
Blondie Fiona	2002 -
Brownie Kaye	2004 -
Black Beauty "Blackie"	2004 -
Betsy Sue	2005 -
Beezus Jean	2006 -
Brandon Phillips	2007 -
Rodger	1999 -2012
Goldie	2006-2011

ACKNOWLEDGEMENTS

I would like to thank some special people I have met since I adopted my first cocker spaniel in 1995. Dr. Brent Pettigrew at Fountain City Veterinary Hospital in Bryan, Ohio, was our first vet. His knowledge was invaluable to these first time dog owners.

After moving to the Dayton area in 2004, we were fortunate to find another wonderful vet. Dr. Larry McKenzie at Englewood Animal Hospital supported us through some difficult decisions as some of our cockers grew older.

After Dr. McKenzie's recent retirement, we entrusted the care of our cockers to Dr. Trent Printz and Dr. Kelsy Printz.

I would like to thank Dr. Lee Schrader at Suburban Veterinary Clinic in Dayton, Ohio, for the excellent care she has given to Blondie. Her knowledge and treatment of canine heart disease has greatly improved Blondie's quality of life.

I would also like to thank the staff of Sunshine Kennel and Garden Center in Union, Ohio. They have provided boarding and grooming services for all of our cocker spaniels over the years. Sherri is the best, most patient groomer ever.

I would like to extend a very special thank-you to Paula Stoll of Paula's Pet Sitting. Our cocker spaniels love Paula, and she takes excellent care of our pack when we are away. I will never forget the day we were out walking our cockers, and Paula stopped her car to talk to us. At the time, we didn't realize we needed a dog sitter. Paula's service has proved to be invaluable over the years.

I would also like to acknowledge two great Ohio shelters - Defiance County Humane Society and Montgomery County Animal Resource Center. We adopted some of our cockers from these shelters. We also worked with these shelters as rescue volunteers.

Finally, I would like to recognize Sue Alandar of furbabiesbysue.com for compiling the group photo of all of our cockers, past and present. Sue has added cockers to the photo as our family has grown over the years.

ABOUT THE AUTHOR

Becky Corwin-Adams was born in Defiance, Ohio. Becky is a wife, mother of two sons, and "MawMaw" to four grandchildren. She currently shares her home with seven cocker spaniels.

As a child, Becky had one cocker spaniel, dozens of cats, chickens, and a variety of "pocket pets." She started writing stories about her pets at an early age. Becky is a freelance writer and columnist for The Farmland News. Becky volunteers for Columbus Cocker Rescue as a foster parent, transporter, and Ebay seller.

Becky has been an avid reader since childhood. She especially enjoys reading Amish fiction, mysteries, and dog stories. When Becky isn't reading or writing, she enjoys crafting and walking with her cocker spaniels. She has had dozens of her original craft patterns published in various craft magazines.

Made in the USA
Middletown, DE
29 August 2022

72544111R00050